Be Sure You Dance

Life's Lessons to help you make every moment count

Stephanie E. Wilson-Coleman

The Empowerment Doctor

The Champagne Connection

Be Sure You Dance

Copyright © 2010 Stephanie E. Wilson-Coleman

The Champagne Connection, Chicago, Illinois
www.champagneconnection.com
www.asipofinspiration.com

Cover design by Borelgraphics

Photographs by SteeleLife Gallery, Chicago, Illinois

All rights Reserved. No part of this book may be reproduced in any form or by any means without permission in writing from the publisher.

The Champagne Connection is not responsible or liable in any way for any advice, course of treatment, diagnosis or any other services or products obtained from the website or written materials. All information presented is for general informative purposes only, and not intended as a substitute for professional medical advice, diagnosis or treatment. Never disregard professional medical advice or delay seeking it because of something you have read in my books, articles or on the Champagne Connection website.

Library of Congress Registration Number: 1-499355261

ISBN: 978-0-9749387-2-1

Printed in the United States

DEDICATION

I dedicate this book to
My mother, Delores Jean Wilson, who made her transition in 2009. May I always make you proud.

To my granddaughter, Imani, be sure to dance.

ACKNOWLEDGEMENTS

I would like to send special thanks and a whole lot of love to my family, friends and fans.

To my Millionaire Mastermind group who supported me and this project through prayer and consciousness, thanks for your encouragement.

To my family who lovingly read every story and shared it with their families, thanks for always being there.

To my friends, who are like an extended family, for trusting in what I believe and participating in numerous consciousness building games

To my readers for demanding that I remain open, honest and prayerful, thank you for your support and confidence in me.

AUTHOR'S NOTES

Be Sure You Dance

In this lifetime, we are presented with a multitude of choices. The choices we make will open doors filled with endless possibilities. Choose the doors you open carefully for this path will affect your life in ways you cannot begin to imagine.

Your choices are and will always be reflected in your human experience. Are you opening the door in front of you because of fear and anger, or are you choosing the door from a place of love and service? Be well acquainted with the emotions that are driving your choices for these will determine the course of your life.

During my life I have made a lot of choices. Some were easy, comfortable decisions, but some were filled with risk and uncertainty. The latter provided the most growth and was well worth any discomfort my ego felt. With each choice, I learned to trust Spirit, the Living One, to listen to my heart and to follow my intuition.

For years, I believed that playing it safe was the way. I followed rules set forth by our society. Rarely did I follow the yearning in my soul. Then my life collapsed around me, leaving me homeless and hopeless. As I worked to rebuild my life, I started to listen to my inner voice. As I allowed my intuition to guide me, I chose to listen to my Spirit. I was able to rebuild my life better than I expected. The only regrets I have were the times I doubted my ability, depended on someone else to make my dreams come true, and believed someone could love me better than I could love myself. When you trust Spirit and dare to believe beyond what you think is possible, magic happens.

I have learned that the only way you can give your faith a fighting chance is to believe in the dreams in your heart and the magic you can create. Feed only the thoughts that inspire; ignore the rest. Surround yourself with people who motivate you, who can extend an uplifting hand to help you climb the mountains in your life. Remind yourself how wonderful you are, forgive daily and rethink what you believe is possible.

As you choose your next experience, I ask that you live like you are dying and remember to dance. Dance with all life has to offer.

"When you are inspired by some great purpose, some extraordinary project, all your thoughts break their bonds: Your mind transcends limitations, your consciousness expands in every direction, and you find yourself in a new, great, and wonderful world. Dormant forces, faculties and talents become alive, and you discover yourself to be a greater person by far than you ever dreamed yourself to be."

—*Patanjali*

"This being human is a guest house. Every morning a new arrival. A joy, a depression, a meanness, some momentary awareness comes as an unexpected visitor. Welcome and entertain all! Even if they're a crowd of sorrows, who violently sweep your house empty of its furniture, still, treat each guest honorably. He may be clearing you out for some new delight. The dark thought, the shame, the malice, meet them at the door laughing and invite them in. Be grateful for whomever comes, because each has been sent as a guide from beyond."

—*RUMI*

Contents

Foreword — xii

Overcoming Blindness — 1

See Spirit in Everything — 5

Ball of Confusion — 10

No Shortage of Growth Opportunities — 15

Wake Up — 19

The Prosperity Game — 23

Easier Than You Think — 28

Changing Your Focus — 33

Visualization — 38

What's Really Going On? — 43

Choose Your Colors — 48

Our Songs — 53

The Road to True Freedom — 57

Changing the World — 61

Slaying the Demons — 65

Stop the Press — 70

Bondage or Freedom — 75

Listening to God — 80

Moving on Up — 84

Always Creating Your Good — 89

Expect the Extraordinary — 94

Ask, Seek, Knock — 99

Doing Nothing — 104

The Best is Yet to Come — 109

The Secret — 114

FOREWORD

Dancing is defined as a series of rhythmic and patterned bodily movements usually performed to music. The dance subliminally involves the management of the pain, price and poise of living our Purpose, modifying our behavior, and developing the life coping mechanisms that work for us.

Again, the dance is usually to music and music comes from the word "muse" which means to think. To amuse is the metaphoric opposite which is to stop thinking. Both have their place in life, but the dance, like music, involves our thought of life. As it is often said: We become what we think most about. Thoughts are powerful, creative and inventive. We dance not only with our bodies, but with our thoughts. Thoughts and images are like magnets, they literally pull us toward them.

I have long believed that experience is not only what happens to us, but what we do with what happens to us.

Wilson-Coleman is a woman whose life reflects the high virtues, values and human validities of tenacity, resilience, and transformational recovery. Her grasp of the universal principles she has learned through her faith and spiritual disciplines are clearly and precisely presented in the brilliant admonitions shared in her writing.

It has been said that the nerve which never relaxes, the eye which never blanches, the thought which never wanders, and the purpose which never wavers—are the masters of victory.

Victim consciousness is the one human fallacy that impedes the progress of the self and soul more than most others. We must learn to be victors over circumstances, rather than victims of them.

Shakespeare said: "Victory is twice itself when the achiever brings home full numbers." It is abundantly obvious in this book that Wilson-Coleman is indeed and achiever and brings home. Life itself is an official school of dancing. Practice doesn't just make perfect, it makes permanent, so be sure you dance and dance to the music (musings) of your own enlightened consciousness!

Peace is possible,

—*Bishop Carlton Pearson*

And David danced before the LORD with all his might.

—*2 Samuel* 6:14 (NLT)

"Forgiveness means that you do not hold others responsible for your experiences."
—*Ernest Holmes*

Overcoming Blindness

I recently attended a Gospel Fest where one of the key songs was "Amazing Grace." The words "I was blind, but now I see," mean more to me now than ever before. I thought back to my experience as a teenage mother, a survivor of sexual molestation and a rape victim. It wasn't until after I graduated from high school, then college, that my vision of "overcoming" my past and washing my mind of memories that sometimes still haunt me today, seemed possible. Poor self-esteem, powerlessness, and unworthiness: these words caused me to remember the importance of *forgiveness*.

I remember first embracing the principle of forgiveness, hoping to change my transgressor. But the more I worked with the principle, my vision, my ability to see, expanded to change *me*, to change my heart. Up to that point of my life, Langston Hughes' *Mother to Son* summed it up perfectly. My life truly had not been a crystal stair; it was filled with tacks, splinters and trauma. But as James Cleveland reminded me, I had come too far from where I started, too far to turn back now, so I kept climbing the mountain no matter how hard it had been.

After intensely embracing forgiveness, ridding myself of spiritual blindness required me to blow up the bridges that connected me to the events of my past. I was no longer mad or angry, but rather, I was definitely finished—finished with unworthiness, turmoil and believing that somehow, as a teenage mother and a survivor of sexual molestation I deserved to be punished. In spite of, or perhaps because of, these events, I had full access to the promises of Spirit. The only requirements were to believe and trust Spirit to handle the details.

The more I embraced forgiveness, the more I felt connected to the Source. This connection became the catalyst for some of the most incredible events of my life. Every drama served as the cocoon for many of the miracles now present in my life.

Embracing forgiveness taught me that once I changed my thoughts and focused on the beauty present within each experience, my reality would become an endless circle of love.

Life is about pushing beyond your dreams and being old enough to believe beyond your limitations.

—Stephanie E. Wilson-Coleman

self-reflections . . .

"I find hope in the darkest of days, and focus in the brightest. I do not judge the universe."
—*Dalai Lama*

See Spirit in Everything

As I began to dissect the "Truth" and become more in tune with the metaphysics of life, I was drawn to A Course in Miracles. Years later, I am still pleasantly surprised at how meaningful the exercises have proven to be, even though I have to admit that as I practiced them it took some time for me to see their value.

One of the exercises that appeared on the surface to be irrelevant and just downright silly ended up being my greatest teacher. As a group of my friends were discussing the Omnipresence of God, one of the women stated that not only is Spirit evenly present everywhere, It is absolutely in and through all things. A Course in Miracles is designed to move us all to the point of understanding what my friend spoke of.

A few of the lessons in A Course in Miracles require you to look at your physical environment and declare that God is in everything. For example, every hour you would look about you and make statements such as: God is in this telephone; God is in this television; God is in this pencil; God is in this lotion, and so on. At first, when I uttered these statements, I would end up laughing as I declared God to be a paper clip, earring or headache. But it was when this exercise prompted me to see God in my pain that I found the true value of this lesson.

A Course in Miracles states that when we are able to see everything with love, appreciation and open-mindness, we will experience the true essence of Spirit. As I continued through my practice periods applying the concept that God is in this headache, my discomfort disappeared. What a revelation! Since my discovery, every time I experience what I conceive to be a challenge, I recall this lesson and begin to see Spirit in the midst of it. Once I started to focus on the All-ness of Spirit, the challenge soon dissipated leaving behind more blessings than I could have imagined.

One of my most recent castle-building experiences involved a speaking engagement. Each time the organization spoke with me about my style and technique, they tried to convince me I needed to change. The organization did not feel

Stephanie E. Wilson-Coleman

I would satisfy the attendees need for entertainment. At the beginning of my short talk, I was so nervous, I felt nauseated. But as I continued to speak and focus on the All-ness of Spirit, the nausea quickly subsided and my session was well received by all in attendance. As a result of this, I received more invitations to speak and was also invited to be a "special" guest on a radio show. Frequently, people who were not able to attend the event have made a special effort to tell me they heard I was fantastic. Not only was Spirit in the midst of this experience, Spirit was powerfully present.

When life is looking a little questionable, boldly declare "Spirit is in this experience" and allow the miracle to occur.

Life offers a smorgasbord of choices filled with unlimited opportunities. Be sure to taste them all.

—Stephanie E. Wilson-Coleman

self-reflections . . .

"Consult not your fears but your hopes and dreams. Think not about your frustrations, but about your unfulfilled potential. Concern yourself not with what you tried and failed in, but with what is still possible for you to do."
—*Pope John XXIII*

Ball of Confusion

Lately it seems to be impossible to pick up a newspaper without reading about financial woes: the housing crisis, unprecedented hikes in gas prices, the alarming rate of mortgage foreclosures, unemployment. People all over the world are caught up in this ball of confusion. Our conversations are filled with downsizing, out of control credit card usage, high fashion clothes in demand, living outside our means. Our minds are consumed with getting, acquiring and searching for free lunches. We crave financial independence; we loathe the discipline it requires. We feel that money is the answer to all our problems, even *Ecclesiastes* 10:19 states money answers everything.

Stephanie E. Wilson-Coleman

In our daily living, we quickly forget that our conversations, thoughts, imagination and feelings serve as the fuel which ignites our manifestations. To put an end to the confusion, we must get back to basics.

Proverbs 18:21 reminds us that life and death are in the power of the tongue. It goes further to state that *they that love it shall eat the fruit thereof.* Because life and death are in the power of the tongue, start by eliminating all negative conversations and comments. Gossip and any form of gossip must end immediately. We have become mesmerized by what we think others are doing, saying, and thinking. This preoccupation has resulted in perpetuating the "little mind" syndrome. While you are minding other folks business, who is minding yours?

Now that you have some free time, I urge you to commit to "minding your business." Identify an area in your financial affairs that you would like to improve. Write down what needs to happen to bring you into alignment with your true financial desire. Now create a mental image and play the "tape" in your head a couple times daily. Paying strict attention to your emotions will guide you through your manifestation. Instead of focusing on money or the actual acquisition of the object of your desire, focus your attention on the feeling you will have when you have reached your goal. At first, your goal should be to hold this feeling for a short while. Work with this emotion until you are able to hold it for longer periods of time. Resist the temptation to decide *how* it will happen. Your responsibility is to maintain the absolute conviction that it *will* happen and sustain the emotion as if it has already occurred. Once you are able to consistently sustain this feeling, you will experience improvement in your financial affairs.

Because receiving is synonymous with giving, you must start to give. While you are preparing for your financial demonstration, many opportunities to return to your old habits will appear. Remember, where you focus your attention your energy flows. In order to remain focused during this incubation period, donate unused items to charities, visit elderly neighbors, volunteer to help a child learn to read, provide financial support to where you are spiritually fed and rejoice in the many overcomings you have already been blessed with.

Happy manifesting.

It is always up to us. Hold on to the pain and trials of yesterday and stay where you are, or, forgive and experience your promised land.

—Stephanie E. Wilson-Coleman

self-reflections . . .

"The fact is, that to do anything in the world worth doing, we must not stand back shivering and thinking of the cold and danger, but jump in and scramble through as well as we can."
—*Robert Cushing*

No Shortage of Growth Opportunities

Anxious to turbocharge my growth, I attended my first "Body Talk" session a few weeks ago. The practitioner was easy to talk to, even though there was not much conversation. She explained the process and I thought "a piece of cake." My first session lasted approximately two and a half hours. The purpose of Body Talk is to reestablish the lines of communication between the body's various energy systems so the body can repair itself and return to its intended state of harmony. At the conclusion of the session, we discussed the issues my body's neuromuscular system revealed to this skilled communicator. I was surprised to learn that my body communicated issues I was not consciously aware of. What an awakening! While I felt confident, my body revealed sadness and fears, that's right, multiple fears. Imagine that. Just when I thought I had it all together. After using prayer treatments for healing, I was instructed to pay close attention to the chain of events in my life over the next fourteen days.

The first week following the session, I was peaceful, calm and grounded. However, on the eighth day, it felt as if all these insecurities just hovered with intentions of staying a while. As each insecurity, fear, sadness, forgetfulness and ill temperedness introduced itself, I found myself unable to breathe.

This experience taught me that we have to work diligently to dig up the graves buried in our subconscious. When you reach a point where you start to feel relaxed, this is the signal to dig a little deeper. Even though we may believe we are unprepared for what we might discover, we are reminded that we just have to jump in and scramble through the best we can. The success is in the willingness and effort to clear out these worn-out, decayed thoughts, feelings, emotions, and memories. There is no requirement for you to clear all of the rubbish at once; the only requirement is to diligently work to clear out the graves. How do you eat an elephant? One bite at a time.

What Spirit wants is our acknowledgement, our consent, our willingness to believe that It lives in us, as us and is *us.*

—Stephanie E. Wilson-Coleman

self-reflections . . .

"You can have anything you want, if you give up the belief that you can't have it."
—*Dr. Robert Anthony*

Wake Up

It seems the saying, "When the student is ready the teacher will appear," has us on "hold," repeatedly asking "How do I change my life? What do I need to do to live my best life now?" We place our lives on pause while we wait for the infamous teacher to appear. As we tarry we fill our idle time with continuous conversations about the imperfections in the fabric of our lives. We replay scenarios of old hurts and relive debilitating disappointments, then wonder why our lives are plagued with financial woes. As we bide our time, seldom do we recall blessings from yesterday, joys of today and anticipated treasures awaiting our discovery in our tomorrows still to come. We fail to remember that where we place our attention, our energy flows. Because it is the nature of energy to create, we unknowingly create turmoil and despair. Where is your attention? What are you creating?

In the song "Wake Up," Harold Melvin wrote "Wake up all the teachers, time to teach a new way." Since it is the glorious nature of the universe to create abundantly, perhaps it is not the teachers who need to wake up, it is each one of us who need to awaken. We are always encircled by abundance and opulence. Any belief in shortage exists in and is created by our consciousness.

The steps to changing your life are easier than we want to believe. To deliberately change your life, improve your health, and conquer your financial nightmares, you must *wake up*. In order to wake up you must start a daily rampage of appreciation. Here is your homework. Daily, that is everyday, for the next 90 days, ask yourself "what do you love about your life?" Verbally state a minimum of five things you are grateful for; make a list of things you can brag about. Also, create a list that includes what you would like to experience. Make sure all your conversations are uplifting and positive. Spend your time talking about what you would like to experience. Stop spending money you do not have and start a financial improvement plan.

As you begin to awaken, your consciousness will change and your life will dramatically improve.

Choose to think beyond the boundaries of your past life.

—Stephanie E. Wilson-Coleman

self-reflections . . .

"If you realized how powerful your thoughts are,
you would never think a negative thought."
—*Peace Pilgrim*

The Prosperity Game

Several days ago, my staff and a few close friends, starting playing "The Prosperity Game." We decided to play the game for thirty days and to record not only our purchases but also our emotions and inner thoughts. The purpose of the game is to expand your imagination and decrease your resistance to the good the Universe has prepared for us and is diligently trying to deliver. However, because of our resistance, It has been unable to do so. I was extremely excited and actually thought I would be able to sail through the game without any adverse thoughts. But this was not the case.

The first day of the game, my emotions ran the gamut from not having enough money to not knowing what to buy. When I did make my purchases, I was concerned if I spent my money wisely. While these emotions caught me by surprise, I was abruptly made aware of areas in my life where my vibration did not match my dreams.

Both Matthew (*Matthew* 7:7) and Luke (*Luke* 11:9) tell us what we ask for we receive, seek we find and when we knock it will open. What is not clear are the required steps for asking, seeking and knocking. During the course of our life, we often ask for prosperity and receive lack, look for health and find illness. Frantically, we search for answers, any answer. We look everywhere, but manage to overlook our thoughts, the culprit of any *dis*-ease we experience. We tend to avoid our thoughts because we want our *life* to change, but *we* do not want to change.

If we are to improve the quality of our demonstrations, we must change our thoughts, our vibrations and our conversations. Knowing this is not enough. After acknowledging the need to change, we must start to demand higher standards of ourselves. Refuse to participate in conversations filled with things you do not want to experience, e.g. sickness, poverty, bad relationships, lack, limitations. Use your most powerful tool—your thoughts—to create the good you deserve, the good you crave. Talk about being financially independent, refuse to gossip and most importantly. attach only positive statements things to your I AM.

The Prosperity Game reminded me that we ask, knock and seek with our feelings, thoughts and words. Guard them with care. Make a commitment to focus on situations, thoughts and feelings that make you feel good. This is the key to success. This is the key to fantastic manifestations.

Remember the blessings of yesterday, dream of the possibilities of tomorrow.

—Stephanie E. Wilson-Coleman

self-reflections . . .

> "Visualize this thing you want. See it, feel it, believe in it. Make your mental blueprint and begin."
> —*Robert Collier*

Easier Than You Think

Everyone, regardless of race, gender or socioeconomic status, lives in a world filled with constant change and uncertainty. The various forms of media we depend upon for information have become a double-edged sword. We are given information to help us maneuver through the upcoming days while simultaneously convincing us there is a shortage of everything we need to have a good life: a shortage of suitable mates, lack of good jobs, rapidly disappearing pension plans and a growing number of teenagers who are a constant menace to our society, and so on. Using this information as a guidepost, we see scarcity in all areas of our lives. The more we accept this as the "truth," the more we watch our lives disintegrate.

Stephanie E. Wilson-Coleman

Our society is filled with examples of opposites. We are bombarded with the lifestyles of the "rich and famous" and made to feel guilty that our names do not appear on any *Forbes* list. We are rocked to sleep by the problems of the extremely poor and reminded that this could happen to us at any moment.

Fortunately, we decide the state of our lives and if we find we do not like the current landscape of our lives, changing is easier than we believe. Contrary to the news reports, nothing is impossible. It does not take a lifetime to change a life. It only takes a firm commitment.

The process necessary to change your life is a simple one. It requires changes in your vision (or "what you see") and your mouth (or "what you say").

No matter how devastating your financial situation, breaking your addiction to negative words, conversations, and thoughts will dramatically improve your finances. Break this addiction by finding something in your life to be grateful for. If you can only find one thing to be grateful for, do not worry. The Universe is not concerned with quantity.

Every day, thank the Universe for the blessings you have received. We are counseled "Because His compassions fail not. They are new every morning." In a short period a time, It will create more events for which to be thankful.

Stop talking about the money you lack and start to praise the money you have. Instead of complaining about your job, give thanks for the job. Remember everyone is an expression of the Creator, even the people you work with. When you endeavor to see everyone in this likeness, all imaginary problems and illusions of lack will disappear.

In order to transcend human tribulations, concentrate on experiencing the moment.

—Stephanie E. Wilson-Coleman

self-reflections . . .

"Nurture your mind with great thoughts, for you will never go any higher than you think."
—*Benjamin Disraeli*

Changing Your Focus

Lately, television and newspapers have been saturated with so much sadness. Stories of people making their transition before they have had a chance to live: tales of wonderful people bought to their knees by illness, or of hardworking couples falling prey to mortgage foreclosures are running rampart throughout our society. These are the events that have us hypnotized and believing that we are victims, unwilling partners in a game headed for destruction. Feeling powerless, we keep telling "stories" of lack, impending doom and financial destruction and if we are not the ones telling the stories, we certainly are intently listening to them and willingly passing them on. We unknowingly weaken our beliefs, or our consciousness every time we participate, actively or passively, in these kinds of conversations. Beliefs are just a set of opinions that we regard as factual. Our "facts" or beliefs about escalating prices, economic disasters and impending illness is the key that activates the various laws of cause and effect. We must learn to change our focus and tell different stories. I often say our conversations and our thoughts must mostly consist of what is right with our lives and less of what is wrong. If you are finding this difficult to achieve, then you must look at what you believe. If you are always sick or think every supervisor you have had treated you unfairly or you are constantly robbing Peter to pay Paul, then your life is speaking volumes about what you believe. It is time for you to focus your attention to your parent thoughts and eliminate them—not gradually, but with deliberate and purposeful intention.

In order to live the life we were created to live, we must start to tell different stories, have different conversations. We all have the same amount of time, how we utilize our time determines our success. The difference between people living their best lives now and people who are not, is consciousness. Because we do not have any time to squander, start right now to think about something that makes you feel good. When you awaken every morning, think of something that happened the day before that made you feel good. Before

Stephanie E. Wilson-Coleman

you fall asleep at night, always think of something that happened during the day that made you feel good. As you begin to focus on good things, you will attract more good things, thereby, giving you material for telling better stories.

We remain needy because we choose to believe in the lies of the darkness instead of basking in the truth of the light.

—Stephanie E. Wilson-Coleman

self-reflections . . .

"To accomplish great things we must first dream, then visualize, then plan . . . believe . . . act!"
—*Alfred A. Montapert*

Visualization

Is there something you really want? Something that makes your heart skip a beat just thinking about it? Something so big, extremely magnificent and absolutely opulent that the thought of it just takes your breath away? Now, close your eyes and imagine that it is yours. You can almost touch it, taste it, feel it. Now open your eyes. Unfortunately for most, after you open your eyes, you conclude that this could never happen for you. My advice to you is to merge your thoughts into a dream. This enables you to live out of your imagination and not your memory. *Webster* defines thinking as "to have in the mind; have as an expectation; dreaming as a visionary creation of the imagination." This is the key to manifestation in its purest form.

Stephanie E. Wilson-Coleman

We have received mandates regarding this readily available tool throughout the Bible: judge righteously, pray believing and think on things that are of good rapport. These are just a few verses that serve as ground rules. Henry Ford says it best: if you think you can do a thing or you think you can't do a thing, you're right.

We have learned that quantum physicists have concluded that everything in our universal plane is interconnected and made up of energy. Scientists have also agreed that we have the undeniable ability to choose how we will respond to the events or dramas in our lives and this action survives as some sort of a conductor to attract items with the same frequency, vibration, to us. So how do we harness this readily available mechanism? The use of visualization, creative or otherwise, is the answer. Because this takes time, you will have less time to spend thinking about negative situations. Start by thinking of something you really would love to have. In your mind, create a scenario, a 2–3 minute video, focusing entirely on receiving this wonderful thing and the feelings you will have after you have received this thing. Make a commitment to view your video several times daily. Sustained visualization will soften your resistance and increase your vibration toward your dream. Once you are able to hold this positive vibration, you will be able to taste, touch and experience the thing that you see so vividly.

Now you are probably wondering how to eliminate the unwanted drama you create daily. Simply stated, the process of visualization can be summed up as faith in action. We must diligently guard where we place our faith. Do you have more faith in "bad economic times" than in the Universes' ability to fulfill all your desires?

Because living out of your imagination is easier than you think, there is no requirement to eradicate anything you are currently experiencing. The requirement is to shift your focus to what you would like to experience. As you spend more time "living in your imagination" you automatically decrease the time you spend "living in your nightmares."

Give it a try.

Strive for a life filled with laughter, a heart filled with love, a body filled with grace.

—Stephanie E. Wilson-Coleman

self-reflections . . .

"Trust your heart, but be quiet for awhile first. Ask questions, then feel the answer. Learn to trust your heart."

—James Earl Jones

What's Really Going On?

Recently, I had the pleasure of attending a metaphysical book club as the members discussed *The Alchemist* by Paulo Coelho.

As I read *The Alchemist*, I was intrigued by one of the conversations the Shepherd had with the Alchemist, where he talked about the conversation taking place in his heart. This prompted me to dedicate a week to listening to, being a witness to the conversations of my heart and my brain.

I teach that achieving any measure of success is dependent upon consistently aligning your thoughts, feelings and conversations. I also teach that meditation is one of the pathways to achieve this.

During the process of serving as a witness to the conversations in my heart and head, I was surprised to discover these conversations were contrary to my true goals. In the business world, if any of your strategies are at conflict, the business will not be successful. This principle holds true for our personal lives for it is written that a double minded individual is unstable in all his ways (*James* 1:8).

As my heart and head volleyed every "what if" scenario possible, I had to resist the urge to interfere. So as a witness, I recorded the thoughts that seem to appear often in the dialogue occurring between these cohorts. This helped me to easily identify the negative beliefs actively engaged in my subconscious. This exercise helped me know what specific items I still needed to forgive and release. I was able to tailor my visualization exercises and choose specific spiritual programs to download into my subconscious.

In our daily quest to achieve our goals, often we forget that mental and spiritual housecleaning must be done continuously. Forgiveness prayers must become a routine part of our life. I also encourage you to take an honest look at what is in both your heart and your head. Do not be surprised to find that the two do not agree. If this is the case, as it was for me, list the items that are the source of disagreement and find the courage to uncover the angst in your own soul. Try writing scenarios that describe the goals you want to achieve. Make the stories vivid, colorful and filled with as much detail as you can provide. This will provide your heart and head with new material to discuss. As you strengthen your visualization you are also giving life to your innermost desires. This will bring your heart and head in agreement.

From time to time, I am overwhelmed by the business of life. The challenges are too frequent and the rewards are too few, but if Life itself is the miracle, then all the things we find in life are an expression of this miracle.

—Stephanie E. Wilson-Coleman

self-reflections . . .

"As we express gratitude, we must never forget that the highest appreciation is not to utter words, but to live by them."

—*John F. Kennedy*

Choose Your Colors

Every moment is filled with all the possibilities life has to offer. One can find happiness, sorrow, joy, sadness. One can find prosperity, poverty, abundance and lack. It is said that life is a canvass and we color it with acts of beauty, kindness, generosity and self-expression. The question we must answer is how do we express our authentic self?

Moment to moment we choose love or fear. We decide if we are coloring our lives and our experiences with peace, hatred, harmony or ill will. I have learned we all have access to the same power. Until we learn to better control our thoughts and stay in alignment with God's will, we will always create a life filled with a smorgasbord of experiences. In spite of the circumstances, we still have a choice.

In today's supercharged world, we are overwhelmed by the number of books filled with useful techniques to help us create a "positive attitude." If you could only choose one, I would recommend the colors of gratitude and appreciation. Using these colors are enough to guarantee you paint a pretty canvas. Staying focused on the good that is continually present in our life requires us to always live in the present moment, in the now while turning a deaf ear to the tales of destruction beckoning for our attention. If you are alive, this magnificently opulent universe floods your life with wonders every hour—become still enough to appreciate these wonders.

Of course when all about us is going our way, appreciation and thanksgiving effortlessly roll off our tongues. It is when the blessings are wearing the colors of darkness, despair, envy and hatred that we are blinded. It is during these times that we have to persist in switching our attention to the good. We have to stay focused on the uplifting colors. Because life is not one dimensional, we can always find something to celebrate. There is always some reason to praise, rejoice. Each experience is filled with something marvelous. Use your vision,

Be Sure You Dance

your focus to find it. You do create your own life, so choose luscious colors.

In all that you may experience—

praise, praise, praise.

Because words are packed with power, utmost caution must be exercised when we speak. Speak only words that heal and inspire.

—Stephanie E. Wilson-Coleman

self-reflections . . .

"The greatest conflicts are not between two people but between one person and himself."
—*Garth Brooks*

Our Songs

As I listen to the songs that fill our churches, radios and mind with lyrics like *I'll pray for you* and *you pray for me* and *watch God change things*, I observe the lives of others. There is a lot of praying, praising and worship going on while deaths from cancer, diabetes, heart disease and poverty increase. The rate of imprisonment of African American males continues to climb and incomes are dwindling at an alarming rate. So I ask for what are we praying, praising and worshiping? If we are what we pray for, what do our prayers say about our life? What do our songs say about our success?

Another song says, if God said it, I believe it. I say, you cannot tell by the conditions of the lives we live. The more we sing and lift Him up, the more we seem to demonstrate the opposite. Why are our experiences contrary to our prayers, praise and celebrations? If the impossible is God's chance to work a miracle, why aren't the miracles showing up in our manifestations? And if we keep fighting will there ever be a victory?

I have discovered that even though our weekly two-hour praise sessions are important, it is what we do with the remaining time that determines the quality, speed and ease of our resurrections and over-comings. We want our lives to change but we do not want to change. Miracles, prosperity, harmony and the other things we pray for will not manifest in our lives until we make definite changes. We must eliminate the hate, outdated beliefs, fear and doubt that we protect and nurture in our own minds. This is the challenge. I say often that every experience we have is our moment of truth. When you are experiencing any conflict, acknowledging you created the event is a good place to start. Once you acknowledge the conflict residing within, get up close and personal with it. Dissect it. Any conflict is a clear indication that you are feeling separated from God. Healing this separation is the key to living the songs you sing.

Our testament to the magnificence of the universe are the lessons we teach.

—Stephanie E. Wilson-Coleman

self-reflections . . .

"To forgive is to set free a prisoner and to discover that the prisoner was you."
—*Lewis B. Smedes*

The Road to True Freedom

During our lifetime we will live several lives, fill several roles. Each experience will leave its mark; but to really open the door to true freedom and start the journey toward true enlightenment, forgiveness is required. Forgiveness is a gift you give to yourself; it is the necessary ingredient to free your inner spirit and untie you from the past.

I know we have all heard this before; however, sometimes we fail to remember that moment by moment we are choosing "who we will serve." When we hold onto any grievance or lack of forgiveness, we are tied to the past. Being tied to the past causes us to "serve and nurse" old events, old patterns, and old stories. The more we live in the past, the more unlikely we are to manifest the desires of our hearts.

You have the tools necessary to start the path to forgiveness or to choose moment by moment to live in the presence of Spirit. Purposely call forth the situation as you remember it. Ask yourself, if the person's true intent was to hurt you; if you made some assumptions that were not discussed; if you assumed agreements that were never made clear. This allows you to step outside of the event and view it from a much broader perspective. After you have done this, imagine what it must feel like to be the other person; imagine yourself having done the same thing. These steps will allow you to recognize how often you find these qualities, actions within yourself. Once you have identified the traits in others that you find to be unforgivable and released them, you can then start to forgive the most important person in your life, *you*.

Because we are all connected, all our thoughts and actions affect each other. Once we can start to forgive ourselves and others, our vibration rises and we are then able to help raise the vibration of others. Each person is our mirror; each moment is our moment of truth. Both serve as bridges to our freedom.

Dancing with Spirit requires constant movement, growth and change.

—Stephanie E. Wilson-Coleman

self-reflections . . .

"There is little difference in people, but that little difference makes a big difference. The little difference is attitude. The big difference is whether it is positive or negative."

—*W. Clement Stone*

Changing the World

Every moment, life prepares and presents to us a smorgasbord of opportunities that entice us to embrace or betray our true selves. If we are not careful, we are lured into comfort, into a place where we readily trade our independence, our ideas, our health and even our self worth for the feeling of security, the ambience of wealth, the illusion of being respected by others. If we are not diligent, we will find ourselves in the same predicament as Judas, selling our beliefs, our spirituality for a few pieces of silver. We find it easier to become absorbed with appearances. We quickly forget who we are and how powerful we are.

Every time we allow ourselves to speak negatively about our finances, money, health, jobs, family, and so forth, we bind our intentions and our vibrations with the creative life force. This will ensure our experiences are filled with lack and limitation. If we persist, our lives, our communities will continue to be filled with crime, poverty and illness. Breaking the spell is critical to our transformation, our resurrection, our success. Because our vibration extends far beyond our physical bodies, we have the power to change the world.

    Changing the world is easier then we believe. A good place to start is to affirm the goodness in life. Most conversations are filled with all that is wrong with our lives. Vow to talk about what is right with your life. The more you affirm the good things, the more the Universe will ensure you have good to talk about. It will not be long before you are experiencing round the clock blessings. Decide who you will serve. We say we believe in God, but all we seem to talk about is "the devil." We do "good" things because we fear the consequences. Start to eliminate any belief you have in dual powers. There is only one power and that power is God. *Embrace change*. Because we must evolve beyond our current existence, change is mandatory. If you live each day as an "adventure," you will give birth to extraordinary qualities. Then you will be able to change the world.

Spirit has planted in all of us wonderful ideas, amazing cures and an unlimited capacity for peace and love.

—Stephanie E. Wilson-Coleman

self-reflections . . .

"Those who have never contacted the Soul will be unaware of the voice of the Soul and will often make the mistake of believing that their emotional impressions are from the Soul."

—*J.J. Dewey*

Slaying the Demons

As we continue to explore spiritual principles surrounding *abundance*, it is necessary to reiterate the formula for success in every area of our lives: thoughts + feelings = demonstration. *Matthew* 5:8 says "Blessed are the pure in heart for they shall see God." *Heart* is defined as one's innermost character, feeling or inclination; the essential or most vital part of something; with deep concern. *Pure* is defined as unmixed with any other matter and God is synonymous with Good.

Over the past few months, I have taught that we ask, seek and knock for abundance through our conversations, our thoughts and our imagination. Because our feelings affect our abundance, improving our emotional state is essential. In fact, our feelings serve as the fuel behind each demonstration. In order to improve your emotional state, you first have to analyze it.

Our society is filled with songs and ceremonies that seem to revere duality. We believe we are blessed and highly favored by a God that some times blesses and sometimes punishes. We are never really quite sure which way the wind is blowing with this deity so we frantically and feverishly "praise His name" all the while feeling a bit apprehensive about what may happen in the future. It is this belief in duality that shows up time and time again in our lives. We are always in need of some type of healing, but when we learn to purify our emotions as well as our thoughts, words and visual images, we will live a life that has a steady stream of abundance, "good" flowing through it. Any *dis*-ease you find in your life is a result of feeling separated from our source—God—which is good all the time.

This separation can be eradicated by changing your emotions. Anytime you find yourself feeling frustration, worried, in doubt, fearful or angry, ask yourself "what am I thinking about that is causing these emotions?" When you have identified the cause, more than likely you will find these very emotions are contradictory to the prayers you pray. We must be in complete spiritual alignment in order to demonstrate the goodness of God. After you have identified the cause, immediately start to think about something that makes you feel hopeful, joyous and excited.

My life has been filled with hard-hat experiences. In order to transmute my emotions surrounding some of the events in my life, I demand better thoughts of myself. I am able to achieve better thoughts by consciously deciding to remember only the good from these experiences. The more you practice this technique, the easier it becomes. Following Paul's guidance to think about things that are honest, just, pure, and lovely will serve as the bridge from dream to reality. As your feeling nature improves, your emotional state will truly be your sip of inspiration.

Because you are the feet, hands and heart of your dreams, it is you who do the work. Vow this day to see only abundance, think only abundance, and celebrate the miracle found within you.

—Stephanie E. Wilson-Coleman

self-reflections . . .

"What we are is God's gift to us. What we become is our gift to God."

—*Eleanor Powell*

Stop the Press

During one of my sunrise Yoga classes, the mantra was "I give myself permission to be kind, loving, healthy and beautiful, just the way God intended me to be." As we intermingled this expression with our rhythmical inhalations and exhalations, I could feel my body experience a charge. I felt a lightness throughout my body and a freedom in my thoughts.

This mantra haunted me so that as the day moved on, I looked at my actions to identify the areas I had given myself permission to experience. Ernest Holmes states in the *Science of Mind* that we only know as much as we can prove by actual demonstration. Using this premise, I looked at my demonstrations.

Stephanie E. Wilson-Coleman

Because I could not resist the temptation, just like everyone else, I looked in the outer first, even though I knew my inner being determined my outer experiences. But contemplating the outer is so much more fun. Here is some of what I discovered.

I have given myself permission to be healthy. This health is demonstrated by maintaining a stable and perfect weight, being committed to a consistent exercise program, wisely managing my food choices and getting adequate amounts of rest. I have a job I love and the future is getting brighter. I finally have a savings plan I cheerfully adhere to and my close associations with people are chosen with the utmost care.

Feeling powerful, I moved to my inner self.

I demonstrate an inner calmness that can handle anything life has thrown my way and life has surely been busy. I have danced with everything from my forecasted death due to an accident, unemployment, homelessness, to brushes with the criminal justice system. In each instance, I was victorious and in some instances, I even dazzled myself. In order to satisfy my craving for extended periods of silence, I increased my meditation time and take long walks. I spend more reflective time writing in my journal. And finally, I bask in the magic of mornings.

Be Sure You Dance

By now I was feeling quite invincible. Since I believe you should not trust your press releases, looking at the not-so-good things in my life was just as important as studying the good. If I was to be true to myself, I had to examine the areas of my life where I had chosen to demonstrate the effects of a lessor vision of myself.

Even though I was prosperous at this point in my life, I knew deep down I could be more prosperous. I was not demonstrating prosperity that would fill my life with extravagant abundance. If I believed in A Course of Miracles, the reason for this, and I had plenty of other reasons, was unadulterated fear. For some unknown reason, I had not given myself permission to be truly successful. Perhaps, I did not trust my own prayers. Just maybe, I felt I did not deserve more prosperity. Or did I think God's will for me was something other than what I had in mind? Because God's will for us is absolute good, I rededicated a portion of my day to working my real dreams so I can prove the omnipotent presence of God in my life. I now understand that proving the power of God in our own life is the real reason for our existence.

Learning to master your emotions is the key to success. Feelings are like highway signs in that they provide information about the things we need to heal in our lives.

—Stephanie E. Wilson-Coleman

self-reflections . . .

"To educate yourself for the feeling of gratitude means to take nothing for granted, but to always seek out and value the kind that will stand behind the action. Nothing that is done for you is a matter of course. Everything originates in a will for the good, which is directed at you. Train yourself never to put off the word or action for the expression of gratitude."

—*Albert Schweitzer*

Bondage or Freedom

Daily we are bombarded with information, evidence and opinions that drive the idea of lack, recession, and poverty deep into our subconscious, leaving us doubting if we are ever going to see the end of high gas prices, rising unemployment and soaring crime. Statistics about the state of our health are out of control. Eight per cent of Americans have diabetes, twenty per cent will die from heart disease and twenty-five per cent from cancer. With the media pushing hopelessness with more intensity than ever, coupled with our willingness to accept it, and as we pass our time envying the lives of the rich and famous, the question is: are we comfortable with our bondage?

We were born to be abundant, prosperous and healthy. *Mark* 11:24 tells us to pray believing that we have received it and it will be ours. *Luke 12:32* reminds us that it is the Father's good pleasure to give us the kingdom. All religious texts make the assumption that God, the Living One, says yes to our beliefs. With this in mind, the most important work we can do is to expose our true beliefs and rid our subconscious of all limiting, poverty-filled thoughts.

People in every religion are quick to speak the word, name it and claim it, but if you look at the results of our demonstrations, I have to ask what are we claiming? Bondage or Freedom?

Freedom is ours; however, we must be willing to pay the price. Because our mental declarations are opposite of what we speak, we must be unceasingly diligent in bringing our beliefs into alignment with our words. It has been proven via quantum physics that we have the power, through our vibratory energy, to change our lives. The beginning steps toward regaining our freedom, changing our lives and our society can be found in 1 *Peter* where we are told the key to life and death is in the tongue and in *Philippians* 4:8 where we are told to think about things that are praiseworthy and of good rapport.

Start now to reclaim your thoughts and words. Think and speak only about those things you wish to experience. Vow to spend more time

Stephanie E. Wilson-Coleman

keeping your mind on your dreams and no time minding someone elses' business. Get back to the basics—start a gratitude journal and find something good to celebrate every day, all day. You will be pleasantly surprised how the universe will thank you.

Let the God times roll.

We must unequivocally commit ourselves to seeing our lives as we are created to be, then with every waking moment strive to live the dreams that were planted within in each of us.

—Stephanie E. Wilson-Coleman

self-reflections . . .

"Just sit there right now; Don't do a thing, just rest. For your separation from God is the hardest work in this world"

—*Hafiz*

Listening to God

As my circle expands, I am always asked "how do I know when I am not in alignment with the will of God?" The usual answer has always been to look at your life; the events of your life will tell you if you are in alignment or not. However, rarely does this give us the tools necessary to adequately answer the question.

My search for alignment has revealed that the voice of Spirit speaks to us in a myriad of ways. Because there is no separation between us and Spirit, the universe surrounding us is filled with telltale signs designed to give us immediate feedback. If we are unable to interpret the information surrounding us, then our bodies and emotions are good places to look.

Any separation from Spirit first appears as signals in the body long before it appears in our relationships, our finances or manifested as ill health. If these are ignored then our emotions will react. So checking in with your body and emotions regularly throughout the day is paramount.

Checking in with the body is a simple task which only requires you to notice how your body is functioning, i.e. any stiffness, tightness, difficulty breathing, etc. Once you have completed the body scan, examine the feelings and allow your mind to return to the first time you experienced the physical feeling. This is the incident that needs forgiveness. After you have forgiven the incident and yourself, then release it. Holding on to old feelings, emotions and opinions will guarantee that the progress you long for will be delayed. Old feelings and resentments will destroy your promise land. This is equivalent to putting new wine into old wine skins. If you are in the middle of an event that is causing the body to send signals of discomfort, slow down and acknowledge the emotions occurring at that moment.

Our mind, our soul have agreed to our divinity. Conflict, which is synonymous with feeling separated from Spirit, occurs anytime our emotions (feelings), thoughts, actions and words are not consistent with our divinity.

The process necessary to change any situation in your life or your business is a simple one. It requires changes in your vision or "what you see" and your conversation or "what you say."

—Stephanie E. Wilson-Coleman

self-reflections . . .

"If you wish to travel far and fast, travel light. Take off all your envies, jealousies, unforgiveness, selfishness, and fears."

—*Glenn Clark*

Moving On Up

This week my life and emotions magnified the first step of the Master Mind Prayer. I felt powerless to solve my own problems and needed help that could not be found in any human being. And of course, after reading one of the daily lessons in a metaphysical magazine that said "I accept my lessons with ease and grace," I felt much worse. Like the Master Mind Prayer, I needed my belief systems completely altered. Because I considered myself to be one of the "spiritually enlightened ones," I did not know what to do or what not to do. Searching for answers in this confused state only led me from one dead-end to another. The confidence and resistance I ran into from others and myself left me punch drunk. So I did what any self-respecting human being would do. I cried, whined, moaned, and complained. In a feeble attempt to find solace, I ran back to the old and familiar, only to discover I had outgrown the experiences, the people, the old haunts and conversations. No matter how much of this I basked in, my soul was not satisfied. Realizing I could not go home, I was now both miserable and frightened. As my grieving started to subside, I was able to identify the problem. I am certain my inner consciousness was relieved and my guardian angels could now relax. Protecting me from my own thoughts, while in this state, had surely been a full-time job.

The past six months were filled with opportunities to mingle with wonderful people and to discuss my brand of "Truth." Jammed packed with trials and triumphs, the cracks in my armor were glowing and without warning, fear moved in and set up house. As my vision became clearer, my passion ignited and this new sense of clarity began to open more doors and lead me down paths that were unfamiliar.

Face to face with the unknown, I no longer could depend on what had worked in the past. Even though this new journey was the answer to my prayers, I began to doubt if I could handle it.

A dear friend of mine uttered the magical words that jarred me from my trance and filled me with renewed vigor. "It's your time." Suddenly I understood. It is our responsibility to live a bountiful life filled with excitement and prosperity. This is our gift to the principle we call God; it is ours just for asking and accepting. In this moment I accepted my good given me by Spirit and continued on my path knowing that Spirit is in the midst of all things. When old man fear creeps in, I remember it is just a "paper tiger" trying to keep me from reaping my harvest.

The next time fear shows up as your companion, know that Spirit is in the midst of all things and get busy looking for your gift.

Our conversations, thoughts, imagination and feelings serve as fuel to spark our experiences.
—Stephanie E. Wilson-Coleman

self-reflections . . .

"Imagination is the beginning of creation. You imagine what you desire, you will what you imagine and at last you create what you will."
—*George Bernard Shaw*

Always Creating Your Good

Ernest Holmes, founder of the Science of Mind philosophy, stated there is no necessity for any negative condition to exist within our bodies other than the necessity we ourselves insist upon. In other words, disease exists within our bodies and negative conditions are prevalent in our lives because we want them to exist.

When I first read this, I immediately examined all the circumstances and appearances currently playing out in my life. Vowing to keep an open mind, I allowed this concept to dance in my consciousness. As I pondered the vast number of possibilities, I wondered why I allow episodes of lack, limitation, and poor health to reappear in my life like a bad made for TV movie. Even though the episodes are less frequent and not nearly as severe as before, nonetheless, they still appear.

I have come to truly understand our reactions are based on love or fear (encompassing their many offspring, such as, jealously, greed, hatred and violence). I could not help but wonder if on some level I was harboring some form of fear. Could I be misusing my "I AM" power by attaching negatives to my experience? Or am I failing to see Spirit in everything? Because we are all perfect creations of the Divine, the whole Spirit of God lives within each of us, creating fertile soil that is dedicated solely to fulfilling our inner most beliefs.

Depending on this power and trusting Spirit to guarantee Its promises, I set out to "love" Spirit much better than ever. Deciding to practice and teach the Goodness of Spirit was very easy. It was the doing that took a bit of effort. I started by correcting the use of my "I AM" power by being consciously aware of the statements I attached to the words I AM. Whenever I became aware of any abuse, I forgave myself and corrected the behavior. When I felt unable to move forward with my ideas, I asked myself, what would I do if I were not afraid? Then I proceeded with the answer. The next thing I did was to see Spirit in, under and a part of absolutely everything. As I blessed the food I ate and the liquid I drank, I did it with awareness that the nourishment was a form of substance and we all know substance is Spirit. As I dressed, I would see my garments energized with the light of Spirit. As I would write, I imagined each word being whispered in my ear and sent forth on the wings of perfect Love.

Because my day is filled with meetings, I would pause periodically to remind myself that everyone present was an Angel and sent to fulfill Spirit's special mission.

Suddenly, small tokens of prosperity began to cross my path. The more aware of these I became, the more I expected them. The Universe did not disappoint me. Soon, everyday was filled with gems of opulence.

Try it. You will not be disappointed.

Until next time, work like you don't need the money, love like you've never been hurt and dance like no one's watching.

You have the power at this moment to change your life.

—Stephanie E. Wilson-Coleman

self-reflections . . .

"Expect your every need to be met. Expect the answer to every problem, expect abundance on every level."

—*Eileen Caddy*

Expect the Extraordinary

I expected today to be a typical day with typical accomplishments, typical conversations and typical decisions. In the midst of what promised to be an ordinary day, an old friend called. When I asked the typical question, how have you been? He replied, *okay, but it is rough; I cannot complain because it is rough all over.* Suddenly, with alacrity, the events of my day propelled from typical to extraordinary. In concert all my senses sang out "things are not rough all over." Quickly my soul agreed. In the next few moments I thought about all the valley experiences and crucifixions of my life—my homelessness, unemployment, sexual molestation, rape and betrayal. With the guidance of Divine Mind, I navigated through this rough terrain and emerged physically healthy, mentally agile and intellectually charged—all in spite of the challenges I created.

In *Working with the Law*, Raymond Holliwell states that the mind is the creative cause of all that transpires in the life of man, that personal conditions are the result of man's action and all actions are the direct outcome of his ideas. If you are not experiencing a life filled with joy, the true problem is the lack of imagination. I prove daily that life gives you what you think, what you expect. Because all things begin with me, in my mind, I achieve everyday all that I believe. At the end of any given period of time, we have demonstrated all we can imagine and believe we can demonstrate.

In order to ensure that everyday is wonderful, I have found that we must do more than guard our thoughts and our actions. Expanding our mind and using our imagination is paramount. We must also carefully select what we read, be choosy about what we watch on television, selective about what we listen to and exercise extreme caution with our relationships. It has been proven that it is easier for someone to convince us of a negative than it is to persuade us of a positive.

Because our mind is the creative cause of all that happens in our lives, be sure to start each day with mental images that support the success you want to achieve. These must be firmly implanted in your mind in order for your actions to be consistent with your desires. If you discover any negative thoughts, see these as the bearer of "useful information." Instead of allowing them to take control of your mind, examine the information they bring and then immediately dismiss any notion contrary to the success you wish to achieve. Of course this is easier said than done, but it must be done if you are to live your dreams.

At the end of this conversation with my friend, I was filled with an exceptional sense of oneness. I knew things are not rough all over; things are exactly as you expect, and I have come to expect my life will always be filled with opulence.

No matter where you find yourself, your mind, thoughts and imagination are the keys for transformation from trials and chaos to victory and success.

—Stephanie E. Wilson-Coleman

self-reflections . . .

"Ask, and it will be given to you; seek, and you will find; knock, and it will be opened to you"
—*Matthew 7:7*

Ask, Seek, Knock

Over the past few months, I have spent a tremendous amount of time thinking about and exploring the principles surrounding abundance. As I work with others trying to help them obtain their goals and express their greatness, I begin to ask what are we really pursuing?

In *Matthew* 7:7 and *Luke* 11:9, we are told "ask, and it shall be given you; seek, and ye shall find; knock, and it shall be opened unto you." We should be mindful about what we ask for, what we seek and where we knock.

Because "the asking" takes many forms, we are often blinded by the actions we are taking, that are giving birth to lack, limitation, illness and poverty in lieu of prosperity, abundance, health and opulence. Many truth teachers often say, If you want to know what you believe look at what you are creating in your life. The universe is designed to fill our lives with "blessings" based on our beliefs, not our prayers. If in the midst of our prayers, we believe in unemployment, bad economies, sickness, disease, and more, while we are praying for prosperity, health and abundance, what we will find evident in our lives are financial problems, illness and lack. Because asking, seeking and knocking is the fuel that determines your manifestations, it is imperative that we work to eliminate any error thoughts we still have and break any subconscious agreements we have made with the physical world. Rev. Michael Beckwith states that manifestation is unavoidable when we are living under cosmic knowledge. Esther Hicks states that we must stop holding the thoughts that cause us to lower our vibration.

To transmute your beliefs so that your manifestations are desirable, you have to stop giving your attention to things you do not want. Start at this moment, refusing to discuss or participate in discussions that solidify old agreements, such as, affirming statements that support financial indebtedness, physical illness, problems due to aging and just being plain ole' tired.

What we talk about, focus on and listen to keeps us in harmony with it. And what we are in harmony with, we create. We must begin to make

Stephanie E. Wilson-Coleman

the connection that what we think about and talk about is creating our experiences, our future.

The next important item in your toolbox is your imagination. Your thoughts conceive the idea, your imagination gives it life. As Flip Wilson used to say: what you see is what you get. Use this power to create clear images that make you feel good in order to manifest what you would like to experience. Instead of imagining what it would feel like if you lost your job, think about what it would feel like if you were promoted. Do not spend any time trying to decide how it will happen; only think about it as if it has happened. Apply this to every area of your life and the results will amaze you.

Just for today, keep your mind filled with possibilities, not obstacles. Just for today, nothing will be impossible.

—Stephanie E. Wilson-Coleman

self-reflections . . .

"Where there is love, no room is too small."
—*Talmud*

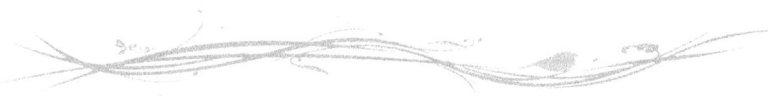

Doing Nothing

How is it possible to start the day with a prayerful consciousness coupled with an overwhelming sense of oneness with the Universe and by evening be filled with a rich assortment of feelings imprisoned by fear, hurt, betrayal and knee-deep in drama?

Because feelings are the traffic signals of life, what message was wrapped in this discomfort? Should I stop, go or proceed with caution. Is it wise to ignore the wave of uncertainty that has eroded the calmness of my soul? Or should I meet this battle head-on like a predator stalking its prey? Both alternatives seemed plausible and the more I contemplated my options the worse I felt. I have often heard when you do not know what to do, do not do anything. Unable to settle on a course of action, I did nothing. Little did I know this would be the best course of action. While following the path of least resistance, I did not expect to be blessed every minute of the day, I did not expect to greet the close of the day eagerly anticipating tomorrow.

My chosen path of idleness served as a sort of healing balm. It soothed all the tender, rough spots I had developed from fighting unnecessary battles.

I took more time with my plants, paying attention to all the new growth. I thanked them for keeping my air clean and providing a source of beauty. I was amazed at how vibrantly alive they were.

I studied the faces of the people I passed on the streets of one of the greatest cities of the world and was showered with smiles, tranquil gazes and eyes twinkling with excitement. As I bid each one good day I, too, shared a smile. I could sense a sort of acceptance, a sense of love of the small gift I offered. Like the little drummer boy, I did not have much to share, but I eagerly gave what I could.

By evening, I extended this idleness to my personal space at home. I listened to old tapes filled with messages that had taken me through a many castle-building experience and later packaged them so I could share their magic with others. I read magazines that had piled up for weeks. Taking my time, allowing myself to indulge in the glamorous, glitzy world of high fashion, was truly a fantasy filled moment. I chose to recycle the magazines by giving them to a women's shelter.

At the end of the day, I sat and watched the various stages of the sunset. I had forgotten just how wonderful it is to bask in the fullness of Spirit.

The next day started just as the previous evening ended, with my soul enfolded in the complete, unconditional love of the Universe.

Joy, inner peace, and tranquility are not dependent upon outer conditions; you have the power at this moment to change your life.

—Stephanie E. Wilson-Coleman

self-reflections . . .

"Whatever with the past has gone, the best is always yet to come"
—*Lucy Larcom*

The Best is yet to Come

Every life is filled with storms and celebrations, chaos and success, confusion and triumphs. During the celebrations, successes and triumphs we boldly take full responsibility for the outcome; but while in the midst of the storm, chaos and confusion we place the blame outside of ourselves. We wonder why "God has forsaken us?" Victim or Volunteer?

In *John* 5:1-9, for 38 years, a man had been faithfully coming to the pool to be healed. Jesus' question to the man was "Do you want to be healed?" The man's response was "There is no one to help me." Many of us model our lives after the man at the pool. When faced with adversity we sit around waiting, begging and crying for someone to help us. We expertly craft excuses for why we are not healed. We have 100 Bible verses at our desk, but we do not believe any of them. Many have become addicted to being sad, sick and tired. We forget that we *decide* our response to everything that occurs in our lives. It is our response that determines the outcome. Because the Universe is benevolent, attitudes of "woe is me" only draw to you more "woe is me" circumstances. You must get sick and tired of being sick and tired.

In order to experience your long awaited healing so that you can live your best lives now, we must take responsibility for all of our actions. No one is a victim; we are all volunteers. If your life is filled with a continuous pattern of similar crisis, this is a sign that you have decided to declare yourself a victim. It is this identification that will certainly guarantee that you will have many more "victim" experiences.

Our reaction to events will also point out where we have placed our faith. If we believe that Spirit is the beginning and end of everything, we must believe completely that Spirit will answer our call, supply our needs and comfort our soul. We are counseled in *Acts* 3:1-26, that it is our Faith (Peter) that does the healing.

You can start to take responsibility for your life by asking yourself "What are my reoccurring crises and dramas?" "What has become clear to me?" Each experience is your teacher, it came to show you what needs to be healed. Once you have started thinking about and answering these questions, record your responses in a journal. Note any similarities. Devise a plan to make the changes your dramas are urging you to make.

Learning to find peace while in the midst of a crisis is the only sure way to calm the storm. While in the crisis, take some time to become still, acknowledge your need and visualize its fulfillment. Follow the guidance you receive. This will shorten the duration of the crisis, keep you positively focused and make certain your Faith is working to manifest the desired outcome.

Everyday find something to be grateful for. If you can only find one thing to be grateful for, do not worry. The Universe is not concerned with quantity.

—Stephanie E. Wilson-Coleman

self-reflections . . .

"Life is a mirror and will reflect back to the thinker what he thinks into it."
—*Ernest Holmes*

The Secret—
The Law of Attraction
You Attract What You Think About

The Secret, commonly known as the Law of Attraction is sweeping the country like a tidal wave. My introduction to the law was in the late '90s. Upon initial awareness of its principles, I could not believe this simple shift in thinking could change my life, but nothing I did prior to this point worked. The fruits of my best thinking produced unemployment and subsequently homelessness. This reality coupled with the residue of being a teenage mother and a rape survivor were teeth-rattling experiences that rocked the calm peace of my soul. I concluded that I did not have anything to lose by giving the Law of Attraction a try.

During the last 10–15 years, scientists have discovered amazing properties and abilities of the brain; at the same time mysteries of the mind have begun to unfold. We have learned that events are processed by the brain, but perhaps, it is the mind that internalizes them

Because of this revelation, ten years ago I committed to practicing this law of 90 days. Due to the amazing, mind-boggling results, I am still practicing the law. These practices have taken me from homelessness to financial independence.

The Law of Attraction (The Secret) is vast, so I encourage you to start with the first two steps.

The first and most beneficial concept is the power of thought. I know, as you read this you are thinking, "I have tried it and I did not see any results." The key to the power of thought are the words you speak. I used to believe that the majority of my thoughts were positive, but when I started to listen to the words I spoke, I was shocked. I said things like "I am so tired" or "I am going on a diet because I need to lose weight" or "I will be happy when . . ." or "I want to be debt-free." Because the Universe (Spirit) is not governed by time nor does It recognize negatives, the Universe (Spirit) heard "I want to be tired; I want to diet; I want to gain weight; I want to be happy later; I want debt." So no matter how positive I thought I was, these things kept showing up in my life.

When I started saying *I am filled with energy and I am financially independent*, I no longer experienced fatigue, my debt was easily eliminated and financial independence is a way of life.

The next concept is to place yourself in circumstances that will increase your ability to act. The Secret points out that even though thought and feeling are necessary to live the life you dream about, it also states that without action nothing in your life will change.

The decision is up to you. In spite of what others consider your shortcomings, you must be in situations that force you to act upon your dream. Everyday, you must do one thing toward the fulfillment of your dream. Start to attend meetings, conventions and talk to someone daily about your plans. Vow to never miss an opportunity to make your ideas known.

In this new millennium, we have fallen prey to instant weight loss, magic cures and overnight successes. In my book, *Embracing Life's Lessons*, I write that when you have been dealt a hard-hat life, you must learn to flex your spiritual muscles. We do a better job destroying our dreams, weakening our will and sabotaging our success than anyone else. We allow our minds to actively participate in flights of fantasy that include flirtations with illness, failure, unemployment and even death. We are often the first to whisper to ourselves, "you can't do this; you will not be successful; you cannot make it by yourself; don't you know the economy is bad?; you can't afford it; you're too black, fat, tall, skinny, white. We have convinced ourselves that it cannot be done by us, and when we fail, we have the nerve to be shocked.

Today, I am your wake up call. We have believed in our burdens too long. If you want to live your dreams now, give The Secret a try.

I have learned that the only way you can give your faith a fighting chance is to believe in the dreams in your heart and the magic you can create. Feed only the thoughts that inspire, ignore the rest.

—Stephanie E. Wilson-Coleman

self-reflections . . .

self-reflections . . .

Other Books by Stephanie E. Wilson-Coleman

Embracing Life's Lessons

A journey to inner peace and tranquility

Is Anybody Listening?

A journey to wholeness

www.ingramcontent.com/pod-product-compliance
Lightning Source LLC
Chambersburg PA
CBHW050645160426
43194CB00010B/1823